Contents

KU-506-949

Beyoncé

Julia Holt

Published in association with The Basic Skills Agency

A MEMBER OF THE HODDER HEADLINE GROUP

The Publishers would like to thank the following for permission to reproduce copyright material:

Photo credits
p.2 © Stewart Cook/Rex Features; p.5 © Kevin Winter/Getty Images; p.8 © Everett Collection/Rex Features; p.12 © Frank Micelotta/ImageDirect/Getty Images; p.16 © DH/Keystone USA/Rex Features; p.18 © New Line/Everett Collection/Rex Features; p.24 © Frank Trapper/Corbis.

Orders: please contact Bookpoint Ltd, 130 Milton Park, Abingdon, Oxon OX14 4SB. Telephone (44) 01235 827720. Fax: (44) 01235 400454. Lines are open 9.00–6.00, Monday to Saturday, with a 24-hour message answering service. Visit our website at www.hoddereducation.co.uk

Copyright © Julia Holt 2005
First published in 2005 by
Hodder Murray, a member of the Hodder Headline Group
338 Euston Road
London NW1 3BH

Impression number 10 9 8 7 6 5 4 3 2
Year   2010 2009 2008 2007 2006 2005

Cover photo © Brian Rasic/Rex Features
Typeset in 14pt Palatino by SX Composing DTP, Rayleigh, Essex.
Printed in Great Britain by CPI Bath.

A catalogue record for this title is available from the British Library

ISBN-10 0 340 90065 2
ISBN-13 978 0 340 90065 9

1 Beyoncé's Dreams

At the age of 11, a girl called Beyoncé Knowles
listed all the things she wanted to do
when she grew up.
Her list was videotaped by her family.

Beyoncé's dreams were very clear.
She said that she wanted to record a gold album
and then a platinum album.
Then she wanted to write her own songs
for her third album.

That young girl grew up and did all those things
before she reached the age of 21.
She made her own dreams come true.

Beyoncé Knowles.

Beyoncé was born in Houston, Texas, in 1981
and her sister, Solange, was born
five years later.
Their Dad, Matthew, was a salesman
and their Mum, Tina, was a hairdresser.

They called their first baby girl Beyoncé.
This was Tina's name before she married Matthew.

At the time no one knew that the shy,
chubby little girl, with the big ears
was going to be such a big star.

2 The Start

When she was little, Beyoncé was very quiet.
When people spoke to her she looked at the floor.
She never put her hand up in class.

At the age of seven, Beyoncé's dance teacher
put her on the stage.
Beyoncé sang a song in front of all the parents
and the other kids.

People were amazed that the quiet, chubby kid
was such a good singer.

When Beyoncé was nine,
she joined a singing group.
They were called Girls Tyme.

The group entered a talent show in 1992.
But they lost and Beyoncé was very sad.
After that, the group broke up.

Beyoncé with her father, Matthew, at the 2004 Grammy awards.

Matthew was sure that his little girl
had a big talent.
So he gave up his job and sold the family house.
He used the money to find a new group of girls
to sing with Beyoncé.
He became their manager.

3 Destiny's Child

Matthew found two girls
called La Tavia and Le Toya.
He put them with Beyoncé and her cousin Kelly.
Together they became Destiny's Child.

Beyoncé's mum chose the name.
She saw it one day when she was reading the Bible.

The girls sang a mix of gospel
and rhythm and blues (R&B).
They wanted to sing like their heroes
The Supremes and The Jackson 5.

Destiny's Child: Beyoncé, Le Toya, La Tavia and Kelly.

Destiny's Child started off small.
At first they only sang at local events.
Then, in 1997, after years and years of hard work,
they got a contract with Columbia Records.

The first song they recorded
was called 'Killing Time'.
It was for the soundtrack
of the film *Men In Black*.

In 1998, they made their first album.
It was called *Destiny's Child*.
It was a big success.
It sold more than a million copies.
Destiny's Child exploded on to the music world.
The girls set off on a big tour
and every ticket was sold out.

The success of their first album was nothing
compared with the success of their second.
It was called *The Writing's On The Wall.*
It sold ten million copies.

From the second album
the group had three hit singles.
The biggest hit was called 'Say My Name'.
It stayed at the top of the charts
for weeks and weeks.

4 The Split

Just as 'Say My Name' flew up the charts,
the group broke up.
La Tavia and Le Toya left.
They said that Matthew
kept too much of their money.

Matthew simply found a new singer for the group.
Her name was Michelle.

La Tavia and Le Toya
took their record company to court.
They didn't like the words to the song 'Survivor'.
They thought it was about them.
They didn't want the song to be played ever again.

Destiny's Child: Kelly, Beyoncé and Michelle.

The words they didn't like were
'You thought I'd be stressed without you
But I'm chillin'
You thought I wouldn't sell without you
Sold nine million'.
In the end, the case was settled out of court.

Nine million was exactly the number of copies
sold of the third album.

5 Going Solo

Beyoncé didn't let the court case
worry her too much.
She had a lot of work to do.
She took more and more control
over the songwriting for the group.

In 2001, Destiny's Child
won two Grammy awards for 'Say My Name'.
Next they recorded a song for the soundtrack
of the new *Charlie's Angels* film.

Later that year Beyoncé, Kelly and Michelle
took a rest from being a group.
They all went solo.

Beyoncé's first solo single
was called 'Work It Out'.
It was for the soundtrack
of the new *Austin Powers* film.

In 2003, Beyoncé chose the songs
for her first solo album.
It was called *Dangerously In Love*.
Some say the album is about her new boyfriend.
He is the rapper Jay-Z.

The first single from the album
has Jay-Z singing on it.

Beyoncé doesn't like to talk about her boyfriend.
They are very close.
The newspapers report that they are looking
for a house together, in London.

Jay-Z and Beyoncé.

6 TV and Film Career

Beyoncé's first career is in singing.
Her second is in acting.

Her first project was a musical.
She sang the lead in a re-make
of the opera, *Carmen*.
It was made by MTV.
They called it 'Carmen: A Hip Hopera'.

Then, in 2002, Beyoncé won a lead part
in a comedy film.
It was called *Austin Powers In Goldmember*.

Beyoncé played a CIA agent
called Foxxy Cleopatra.
In the film, Foxxy and Austin Powers
have to save the world
from Dr Evil and Goldmember.

Beyoncé as Foxxy Cleopatra in *Austin Powers In Goldmember*.

Goldmember was a very successful film.
Beyoncé proved that she had acting skills.
With a hit film behind her,
she soon started to get lots of other film offers.

In 2003, she chose a part in the film
The Fighting Temptations.
The film tells the story of a man who has to
make his local gospel choir a success.
If they are a success
he will inherit lots of money.
Beyoncé plays a gospel singer who saves the day.

Sadly the film flopped.
It didn't make much money.
One unsuccessful film did not stop Beyoncé.

In 2004, she started work on another film.
This time it was another comedy.
It was a re-make of *The Pink Panther*.

It was filmed in Paris.
In the film Beyoncé plays a sexy singer.

In the same year Beyoncé was chosen to be
the new voice of Pepsi.
She got the job when Britney Spears'
contract ended.
Beyoncé made a Pepsi advert with Pink and Britney.
All three of them were dressed as gladiators.

Beyoncé is also the frontperson
for L'Oréal adverts.
She seems to be just as happy acting
as she is singing.

7 Today

Today Beyoncé lives in a big house in Miami.
When she's not working, she likes to be at home.

When Beyoncé wants to relax she lights candles,
plays jazz and paints pictures.
Sometimes she paints all night!

In the summer of 2004,
Beyoncé was sent for by Prince Charles.
He is a big fan of hers.
He wanted Beyoncé and Jay-Z
to sing at his Prince's Trust Music Festival.

After the festival, Beyoncé and Jay-Z
went to dinner at Buckingham Palace.
The Prince wanted to say thank you to them
for all their hard work.

After a holiday in the sun,
Beyoncé got back to work.
Kelly, Michelle and Beyoncé
started to record a new Destiny's Child album.

It's their first album since 2001.
Some of the songs from their new album
were part of a Pepsi TV show in 2004.

8 The Future

In 2004, Beyoncé won five Grammy awards.
At the awards show she wore a sexy gold dress.
The dress was made from her mum's design.

Beyoncé and Tina have a plan for the future.
The two of them went to all the big fashion shows
in Paris, New York and Milan.
They were doing their homework.

They want to start designing fashions
that kids can afford.
This will be a third career for Beyoncé!

Beyoncé at the 2004 Grammy awards.

Beyoncé has done all the things
she said she would do when she was 11.
In fact, she has done much more.
Now, she has a new list of things she wants to do.

Beyoncé wants to go to university.
She also wants to be the first black woman
to win an Oscar, a Tony and a Grammy.
These are film and music awards.

There seems to be no stopping her!

9 Beyoncé Quiz

1   What did Beyoncé want to do
     when she grew up?

2   Where was Beyoncé born?

3   What was the name of the first group
     that Beyoncé joined?

4   What was the name of the first song
     that Destiny's Child recorded?

5   How many copies were sold of
     Destiny's Child's third album?

6   What was the name of Beyoncé's
     first solo single?

7   Who is Beyoncé's boyfriend?

8   In which film did Beyoncé play
     Foxxy Cleopatra?

9   What adverts has Beyoncé appeared in?

10   How many Grammy awards did Beyoncé
     win in 2004?